STEPHEN SONDHEIM
BROADWAY SOLOS

T0085051

CONTENTS

THE CD IS PLAYABLE ON ANY CD PLAYER, AND IS ALSO ENHANCED SO MAC AND PC USERS CAN ADJUST THE RECORDING TO ANY TEMPO WITHOUT CHANGING THE PITCH.

ISBN 978-1-4234-7279-7

RILTING MUSIC, INC.

EXCLUSIVELY DISTRIBUTED BY

HAL•LEONARD®
CORPORATION

7777 W. BLUEMOUND RD. P.O. BOX 13819 MILWAUKEE, WI 53213

Visit Hal Leonard Online at
www.halleonard.com

ANYONE CAN WHISTLE

from ANYONE CAN WHISTLE

ALTO SAX

Words and Music by
STEPHEN SONDHEIM

BEING ALIVE
from COMPANY

ALTO SAX

Music and Lyrics by
STEPHEN SONDHEIM

BROADWAY BABY

from FOLLIES

5/6

ALTO SAX

Music and Lyrics by
STEPHEN SONDHEIM

CHILDREN WILL LISTEN
from INTO THE WOODS

7/8

ALTO SAX

Words and Music by
STEPHEN SONDHEIM

COMEDY TONIGHT

from A FUNNY THING HAPPENED ON THE WAY TO THE FORUM

9/10

ALTO SAX

Words and Music by
STEPHEN SONDHEIM

GOOD THING GOING

from MERRILY WE ROLL ALONG

Words and Music by
STEPHEN SONDHEIM

ALTO SAX

JOHANNA
from SWEENEY TODD

ALTO SAX

Words and Music by
STEPHEN SONDHEIM

LOSING MY MIND

from FOLLIES

ALTO SAX

Music and Lyrics by
STEPHEN SONDHEIM

NOT A DAY GOES BY

from MERRILY WE ROLL ALONG

ALTO SAX

Words and Music by
STEPHEN SONDHEIM

Slowly, with feeling

NOT WHILE I'M AROUND

from SWEENEY TODD

Words and Music by
STEPHEN SONDHEIM

ALTO SAX

19/20

Molto rubato

OLD FRIENDS
from MERRILY WE ROLL ALONG

ALTO SAX

Words and Music by
STEPHEN SONDHEIM

PRETTY WOMEN

from SWEENEY TODD

Words and Music by
STEPHEN SONDHEIM

ALTO SAX

SEND IN THE CLOWNS
from the Musical A LITTLE NIGHT MUSIC

Words and Music by
STEPHEN SONDHEIM

25/26

ALTO SAX

Slowly, with feeling

SUNDAY
from SUNDAY IN THE PARK WITH GEORGE

Words and Music by
STEPHEN SONDHEIM

ALTO SAX